ALAS NEW YORK

Poems 2004-2006

Jefferson White

ISBN 978-1-84753-443-9

Associated website
litwit.org.uk

This is the First Edition of ***Alas New York***
Typeset in Times New Roman
2007

Published and printed by lulu.com:

http://www.lulu.com

For Donald Rumsfeld, the man whose "...unknown unknowns — the ones we don't know we don't know..." have done so much to put the laughter into slaughter;

Contents

Refusing to be Obscure

Poetry today? You know what to expect. The main publishing houses set the style and then adhere to it as if it were something other than their own creation. Poetry today is image based, concrete, demonstrative rather than didactic, often culturally parcelled out into acceptable chunks: local, dialect, ethnic, sectarian or anti-sectarian. It is often full of itself and often too full of self. It can be like meditation without a navel. Some of it is good and will be remembered; most of it is drivel.

But that is what we see, for it is what we are allowed to see. There is a much bigger category. That is poetry without the "today": simply poetry, the use of language in formalised patterns to communicate. Jeff White communicates with wit, often didactically. He likes rhyme, puns and word games. He is at times angry, at others despondent; he is frustrated and celebratory, and he does all this through verse in his own way.

What a relief to read someone who doesn't give a damn about keeping in line with the times. Who is careless about being PC and careful about how he says things that mean something to him. Jeff White is not the poet-cypher that so many of us become as we submit our work to the scrutiny of groups, editors and the follow-my-leader culture. He says what he has to say and then moves on. He is not into the whirlpools of inner meaning in which the writer readily drowns. His philosophical grounding is far too rigorous to allow swimming through language without landmarks that we can all readily identify and upon which we rely for everyday discourse.

Another welcome feature of Jeff White's poetry is that he will make you laugh. A poet who is not afraid to be funny is a courageous thing. Laughter is perhaps too infrequent in most areas of modern life but in the world of poetry, it is a raindrop in a desert. All the words that often mock or knock – words such as witty, trivial, teasing, sarcastic – can be used about Jeff White's poetry but used as praise. These are unashamedly bold, brassy constructs laid down from a heart and mind that has looked longer and harder than the mood and tenor of times would easily allow. So read his poems, and then read again.

John Hudson
Quillet
Castle Douglas
2007

John Hudson is a poet and installation artist with an international reputation. He has worked in France, the USA and China, as well as the UK. He is the Editor of *Markings* Magazine.

Author's Apology

As it seems to be the in thing to do these days, I wish to apologise. There is this problem, you see, as to whether to use an "s" or a "z" when apologiszing. Some say that it's an "s" when one is in Scotland and a "z" when one is in North America. Others say than it is wrong to say "one is" when "I am" is meant, unless one is the Queen, of course, when one uses onces far more often than ices.

In all such cases id is advisable.

I would never have managed except for the limited number of rhymes there are in this world, even though they are almost miraculously varied by regional accents, mispronunciations, half rhymes, part rhymes, and such like in all the dialects, vernaculars, argots, lingos, and patois which are going about these days. But all that is just an excuse, and I don't want to make one of those. Also I don't like upper case letters very much. And that photo of me on the back cover— "Well I never!", as my great-auntie used to say, though not recently, because she is dead.

Sorry.

— Jeff White

April 2007
Craigcroft
Laurieston

ALAS NEW YORK

The Death of Optimism

i no longer want to hear current events
the news is as bad as when i first made sense
of it fifty years ago, much happened since
some has improved: the science, the stench
has lessened where i live, but then there's the bench
laws have become more repressive, and wars
have not decreased in frequency or their horrors

so as my grandchildren heave into view
the pot goes on boiling, the old stew's abrew
Candide's in his garden with Pangloss and Cunegonde
the world's gone to hell and the news it goes on and on

The Technical Prescient Bush

if we want to stop air pollution
and purify all the true breeze
africa, the subcontinent
both have to go
and so do the indo-chinese

yup, that just about
should clear it up;
'cept for russia
and the middle east

only latinos will then foul the sea
but, hell, they're our mates
so jus' leave 'em be

besides when the world
has all been made good
we'll need an enemy
won't we then, dude

someone we all know quite well
and distrust
latinos will do it
believe me on this one

i am your president
i am george bush
stem cells can't attack you
i gave them the push

so this global warming
with all of its tricks
cannot survive my
technological fix

Democracy

carping, endless carping
that's what we humans do
truth, beauty, and goodness
are rarely in our view

for we are busybodies
what'er we may pursue
interfere with everyone
else keeping tabs on you

it's their/our job, observers
of the antics of the free
liberty applies to all
never to you or me

for all that we may try our best
the most are anti, and won't rest

Ach weel,
the Auld Art Toon Does it Agin

some momentous Franco-American art
has come to Kirkcudbright
a bit of a lark
it hangs in the Tolbooth
where in days of yore
highwaymen dangled
to settle their score

but now it is art
suspended on halters
abstract, no doubt,
up there on the altars

hoisting aloft
the twentieth century
showing no sign of new epoch adventurey

**The Auld Enmity
and How to Revive It**

a million billion midges
once at ninety decibels
the sound of Scotland resisting
despiséd foreign swells

but now there's been invented
an invidious machine
which kills a trillion midges
with its pheromonal scream

ingeniously a vacuum bag
attached beneath a cream
enamelled chimney down which
hordes of midges stream

to die when they're electrified
in scents not what they seemed
around them happy Sassenachs
their holidays redeemed

Scotsmen, rise inspired
by this curse of yesteryear
and seek ye a new weapon
something Englishmen still fear

Local Cooling

it's April showers
that bring May flowers
and clouds of rain
          to fall on June

July's deluges
are centrifuges
twirling up
          August's monsoons

September forms
October's storms
November's freeze
          arrives so soon

that grey December's
inclement weather
portends a whole new year
          of gloom

Time for Damsels

st george schlepped the schloch
slaying the dragon
untying maiden from her rock,
slipped her the shmok upon the wagon home

arriving late
eight of the clock
they would have had
to go to bed
without their nosh

but having fed
again they bred
and did no wrong, for
maidens don't last long
in epic song

even without kakameyme yiddish
no one can do myth quite like the British

The Judge who Thought his Victim 2/3's of a Cat

... you will serve six consecutive life sentences,
in solitary confinement, without possibility of parole ...

"May you suffer sixty times as much
as did that bat you paddled
when (poor innocent) it lit
on your wife's hat

or the cat you shot with a bb gun
when it sat upon the mat
with a sparrow hawk between its claws,
now what do you think of that?"

"Guilty, your honour, even though
the sparrow hawk had killed
six robins, three greenfinches,
and a half-a-dozen crows

or that that cat had murdered
forty voles in fifteen days,
I think (if reconsidered) guidelines say
it's thirty days."

"Aye", the judge relented:
"agreed, and so it is,
that means we owe you eighteen years
remand, so go about your biz."

"Thank you, sir, but compensation?
all these years that is,
that I have not been working
for my wife or for my kids

they've all grown up now
she's divorced me
and I missed their youth"
The judge he thought "forsooth!"

and then

"Six life sentences I say
as I did before; the nation can't afford
your plea:
begone! forevermore."

Yet Another Initiative

arabs and israelis
are pushing up daises

cellphone to france
if you want in the dance

there's condi rice
if you hope to look nice

telephone the UN
if you want to delay again

syria's most serious
if you like the delirious

or there's iran
mebby even there's pakistan

if catatonicity
try international duplicity

prefer aplomb
there is always the atom bomb

Fellow Alumni

gosh how many have taught school
following the golden rule
that what unto us has been done
should happen to everyone

how else could yesterday's mistakes
be transmitted
the world awaits

The Death of Freud

i saw the green flash, and cut it in half
i did, o i did, o i did

inside of it were Jonah's old bones
and a couple of half-tons of squid

a whale of a time i was having, i said
but what will become of my id?

id will go after the super-ego
and succumb to the highest that's bid

Sigmund had told us, he did, o he did
until after we'd screwed down the lid

when to our attention it was brought to mention
he thought of himself as El Cid

but Vienna had turned
while Valencia had burned

though neither should dampen the squib
which may just go off while you're having a cough

(if you're looking for punch lines
ad lib)

Argument for the Next Crusade (Number Thirteen)

well that's the last bastion
of honour to fall
Pakistan loses runs
for tweaking the ball

to make matters worse, they
go off in a huff
we have no choice but
for cutting up rough

we fought the last war
in defence of the empire
we'll fight the next one
deference to the umpire

there are worse reasons
for going to battle
at least this the latest one
puts paid to prattle

rebut the rules
of this the great game
and you shall lose more
than just your good name

the cause it is just
and our swords surely rattle
give in to the rules
or be slaughtered like cattle

oops, so it's costing us
ten million quid
so we'll back off now
and just stay timid

The 100.00% Poll in Iraq

It's statistically likely
some certainly say
point one percent died
while on their way

to tick on their ballots
and once again pray
that Saddam is Allah
and so he should stay.

It's not that he's bright
or suffers good looks
it's just that he writes
the only read books.

No thousand and one
Arabian Nights,
No Scheherazade could
survive his delights.

As a reward
he has let out of jail
all the cut-throats and rapists
to re try their trail

so better we all
this side of the tomb
conceal reservations
which lighten the gloom.

It's statistically likely
some certainly say
point one percent died
while on their way...

so all is not lost
there may be some hope
but I wouldn't bet on it
at these odds. Nope.

Junket Governance

What greater depths be there to plummet
than world leaders at a summit
what temptation makes them all
raise our taxes as they fall?

O' mortal hand! what eye could sway
them from impinging on our pay?

What little each man has to give
is filtered out in the great sieve
and is assigned as was before
to shrill pursuit of the next war?

This time it looks like Muslimism
is to get the great big schism
smart bombs think when you parade
make no mistake: this is crUSAde.

Homeland Security

the one hundred thousand
nine hundred and ten
plus some dozens more
too secret to men-

tion, all of these agencies
reduced to one
the Knights of George Bush
o now we'll have fun

Ol' Betsy from Fright

I got three daughters
and seventeen sons
and forty five cents
and I says it was

no attack on Iraq jus'
an' purely because
my momma won't get medi-
cade if I does

should she resusci-
tate then all'u'd be done
she'd come back home 'n
Usama'd've won,

'gainst my twenty pistols,
an' Baby Ruth bar
which are all that I got to keep
him from my door

if you gonna let in
this Bin Laden man
you better shut off
my TV or you'll land

upon my airport
I don't want no war
we got no twin towers
down here anymore

we strung 'em all up
from a high hangin' tree
where to regard what
America see

and if you think lynch mobs
is all that we be
then you ain't seen Waco
or Timmy Mc V

Enjoying the Light

how big is our small
how happy our sad
how "good enough"
is sufficient "too bad" ?

how far away
is "so close" and "too near"
why in perfection
are flies in our beer?

what past has the future's
prediction so soon
nurtured and natured
this braw afternoon?

if you have history's
mystery's to fear
remember this evening,
we made it, my dear

The Research Grant Application

go, glow
frightfully blow
globally warmed
by the coming ice age

hop, bow,
apocalypse now
or take up new duties
amazed

be prudent, O
my researching student:
and fill up the next fifty page

if this grant don't come
we are thoroughly done
and will have to do science off-stage.

The Observer

i watch while
the world goes by
it gets no better
nor do i

The Twentieth Century

i was raised in a wondrous time
when all the superstitions pined
suppressed by men but men must be
more vicious than the dreams they flee

and now it ebbs, the wondrous tide
the empirical old men have died
and superstition's back to be
inheritor of history

religion's run by men of sorts
obsessed and damned, beyond recourse
they make the Meccas, Vaticans
and claim the dead Jerusalems

i was raised at a wondrous time
when freedom flared, short fused, sublime
i hope i do not live to see
the new dark age which is to be

Obi's City's Moking

Why is it that trees are blue?
Why is lipstick green?
Why does it cost a quarter
more than it used to have been?

Why is it that grumpy olds
are on the TV seen
when once we had them happily
around the fire screen?

Why are all the bad old days
replaced by what's now good?
The baddies were much nicer and
we knew they understood.

But "times have changed" as walrus said
(he talked of many thing)
of health and safety and respect
for evil's on the wing

Another day another dollar's
made by changing fashion.
These things never used to happen
back when sweets were on the ration.

Temperance

On Christmas day no reindeer play
for they are too damn tired
the strain of pulling Santa's sleigh
has made them hot and ired.

Half a billion households
full of mince pies ate apace
and tuns and tuns of sherry dregs
which Santa couldn't face.

So go enjoy your turkey
while the reindeer bless you all
they're glad you don't eat jerky
Merry Christmas one and all!

The Knight before Crispness

there's a storm in my teacup
ice floes in my gin
globally warmed by the
asteroid's bim
and the bang when it landed
last far out of doors
annihilating all
of the small dinosaurs

the big ones are left
they're descending in droves
their giant wind turbines
swipe air as it blows
one can't light a fire
because CO_2 grows
or even perspire
lest ozones stop snows

while taxes and surcharges
rise out of sight
sugar plum fairies
get aired every night
all the sceptics are hung
from blocked chimneys to spare
any alarmist wisdoms
from meeting fresh air

Boxing Day

Santa Claus knows that his elves
do not like the light
in summer they make video games
till ten o'clock at night

in winter they make barbie dolls
and never stop or fight
on Christmas day they hurl them
down chimneys through the flight

he's never had to pay them
they were always out of sight
(capitalists kept unions down
this was their major might)

but now EU directive
eight nine three (the work ethic)
has forced poor bloody Santa
into consulting the Vedic

the thirty hour working week
has entranced every elf
production's slowed: no Christmases
post two thousand and twelve

that's the way it goes, O Santa
European laws
no one detects the troubles till
they're caught up in the flaws

The Quest for Certainty

i think that anyone can see
a glorious philosophy
but better than to shout about it
is, ineluctably, to doubt it

On Watching the Hills Burn

I wonder how the weather
whatever it might be
confers upon the heather
such inflammability?

No emperor or president
or king or high mufti
could moot unto those roots
signs of enduring enmity.

Yet perchance there's happenstance
so why don't you and me
belie the blame and help reflame
the lamps of history?

A fiery blaze might shift the phase
which curried yesteryear
and biryanied Sundays
on the barbecues of fear.

There's little joy in sorrow
for tomorrow has moved out,
there's farthings left to borrow
from the bankers of true doubt.

One wonders why the whether
whatever it may be
confers upon the heather
such inflammability?

Sic Transit

a gliding down a glacier
one cold summer afternoon
the moon-set shone like pristine dawn
on lawn, long lorn of loon

the breakfast fork and knife and spoon
ascending by balloon
remind me one day Chinamen
will land upon the moon

but lo, there is a buck to make
in the downtown saloon
what better fate awaits the snake
beneath the gonfalon

a gliding down a glacier
apres ski, with macaroon
to side-step and upset the rocks
where druids once chipped rune

the yes, the know, the wheretofore
the lyrics for these tunes
in truth, tomorrow's yesterdays
were writ by picaroons

the elephants up in the Alps
with Hannibal survived
at least until that foetal day
an avalanche arrived

in knot betwixt the tying
and the sword-slice which contrived
Alexander's rise and fall
an umpire may have sighed...

that is how it seems from books
where progress cocks its snooks
but when you're gliding down a glacier
backwards, no one looks

The Doorstopper

old Mother Hubbard
sat in south London
eating granola and whey
along came Greenpeace
who sat down to fleece
her of all her pension right away

'twas in a good cause
reduced methane emissions
they installed the fart stoppers that day
and old Mother Hubbard
blew up in her cupboard
but world warming was kept at bay

The Postmodern Priesthood

how can we have cosmology
which won't say how came we
mathematical theology's
more like it: none can see

through the abstruseness of the verbs
and nouns of nothing be
go back to work, you physicists
attach reality

The Moving Ass

O Saddam Who's Sane
how evil your star
as febrile as even
our Tony Blair are

but can their be useless
like George Walker Bush
who, flushing the toilet,
cannot find the brush?

The Aftermath of Holy War

Saddam Hussein
once ruled Iraq
now someone's disposed of him
I'd like him back

not wealth and not freedom
not democracy—
someone to keep neighbours
from shooting at me

The Lurgie

i thought you were
ashore at first
but then i could not see

that anchors had been
dropped, of course,
and you had fled from me

away, away the you did stray
far flung from distant C
so high that no soprano'd
hit it, even after B

tides go in and tides go out
milk springs from every T
it flows forever from its nose

gesundheit by the sea

Old Folks Nursery Rhyme

Jack and Jill went to Boghill
a standard Comprehensive
Jack passed out
Cambridge did tout
and Jill became streetwalker.

Jack did snitch for MI6
and Jill became a business
but when it came
to pension time
neither emerged with finesse.

Jack's on fifty grand a year
while Jill's a mere stakeholder
reliant upon
state hand outs
(this comes with getting older).

If they'd known when they begun
how down
the upside tumbled
they'd both have realised the fact:
the tax man has you rumbled.

Now the two have come to rue
beneath
the towering charges
which Eventide Rest Homes' excise --
such futures one must ponder.

Girl on Top

the ceiling is revealing
underneath the atmosphere
but nothing's so appealing
as the rest of you I spear

the up the down the all around
the head of you, the rear
and then there's the inside of you
my love, my cheer, my dear

Arthropods

the ants are marching side by side
three up and three opposed
like cars upon a motorway
they slow, they race
it flows

but then a regulation falls
and traffic cops in pairs
circumambulation stops
procedures come to bear

we learned it from the insects, this,
how to set up the snares
and nowhere now but mountain tops
can man do as he dares

In Mem J.B. Hatcher

triceratops is not quite
the dinosaur we thought
computer simulations now
have made him as he ought

of all the ways of telling lies
computing's to the fore
it beats prevarication
and the wiles of Elsinore

so if there is a mystery
or case you've yet to prove
computer simulation 'd be
an excellent next move

Blunt Instruments

i had a molar but it grew
became a wisdom tooth
it had to be extracted
when impacted at the root

so mind ye, mind ye how ye go
and ne'er speak in doot
for acorns from great oaks descend
in their Doc Martin boots

to dunt the mind withoot within
suspicious of the truths
this only can be cured by pots
of chicken noodle soup

In Mem Johnny Cash

when you are travelling
down lonesome roads
don't save princesses
who turn to toads
love is not senseless
it feels and hears
and says princesses
cause endless tears

so only stay
to be sublime
if you're up for it
i've got the time
rubbing a nose
like the Esquimaux
or clipping nails
off the ingrown toes

she loved me cruel
she loved me fine
she used my wallet
to tell the time
when time ran out
and the money thin
she found a better
way to sin

so only stay
to be sublime
if you're up for it
i've got the time
rubbing a nose
like the Esquimaux
don't bare your flanks
to the mosquitoes

Epitaph upon Walking the Boards

ineptly i grew
  two heads and a tu-
    tu forever to live on the stage
      unluck meant i leapt
        but never connected

with what was to be all the rage

so now i'm near dead
  it was nothing to dread
    being dealt all my cards by the stars
      a life in a riot where nothing would buy it

at least i escaped selling cars

God Shedding Grace

how could there be America
without a war or two?
if no one crawled or cowered
whenever you say boo?

Philosophical Investigations

How very strange that the track of this twaddle
lies so far beneath the dregs in the bottle
why o why o is there no one to come
to fill up our glasses when we need more rum?

Progress

once we threw our litter on the ground
a little man with few employment prospects
swept it on

once we blew down spittle
gum, and human stuff
and then the little man he came along and scraped it up

now we get spot fines for this
although the streets stay filthy
but highly paid hygienists say it's much more healthy

the street sweep man is in day care
attended by professionals
and lucky he's to have them, 'cause the rest of us are amateurs

everything is "better run"
the no brained little job is gone
and no one sees that we've gone wrong

The Bells of Hell

dong-dong-dong-dong

pickles and relish
sunday bells are so hellish
i want to go
to where this is not so

ee-en-yalla-djinnn-eskenett

it's the muezzin in the minaret
by megaphone gets his message sent
his ghetto blaster
puts 'em down so much faster

rows upon rows
of the mindless in throes
farting at gods
while they're kissing the clods

where's the escape
from the power of the flake?
't must be in an afterlife
where this madness is not so rife

meantime we mortals
reservedly mouth our chortles
but back comes the gong
and more muezzin

this can't last long
dong-dong-dong-dong

He Equals MC, Squire

the fundamental flaws of physics
all its gravitas
phenomenon phenomenal
Darwin and, alas,

evolving creationism
big bang, not the Word
atom over Adam
is a monkey so absurd?

and then we have Mohammet come
to upstage Jesus Christ
with seventy two virgins
in his heaven, aint that nice

compared to harps and singing
its Mohammet gets the votes
if only pre-arrival
didn't involve slitting throats

so let us stick with science
as once we did with nurse
for otherwise religion's there
to offer something worse

Persistent Vegetative State

persistent vegetative state
i thought that meant George Bush
but no it means some smiley lass
who's being guv the push

her time has come she has to go
they love her very much
and so they dehydrate her
and then starve her as a crutch

she's not put down like a sick dog
or timothy mcveigh
they kill her like some worthless frog
who's overstayed it's day

how can we be so cruel
to ourselves in this mad way
we're only kind to animals
or buggered weans today

a pope is going to die tonight
i sense testosterone
as colleges of cardinals
fight to grasp the bone

easter's one hour less this year
the rebirth is foreshortened
and we'd best only fear the tear
our wise men have contorted

On Casting my Vote

all of our voting is tactical
none of the outside can win
so when you pretend
free will's placing your cross
you’re committing a venial sin

not having turned democrazy
but not really letting it in
there’s freedom to vote
but no freedom of note
has ever this way been let in

do you want to be ruled by others
do you want to be ruled at all
there is no choice once the crosses go down
you are going to be ruled
it's their call

if you want to make your decisions
and do not want others involved
then you must resist
the vox populist
and ignore whatever they've scrawled

there is no argument that’s for freedom
there is no argument against law
for law’s what pretends
that the thoughts of your friends
can mean anything more than fuck all

LBJ's Advice to Gerald Ford

not having been a pacifist
but lived a while, i'll tell you this
nothing removes bully's wrist
faster than a bit of fist
do not eschew the martial arts
man must chew gum before he farts

The Lost Arts

away into the sky so high
the levitatee flies
on wire and strings and spindly things
where faker's spelt with "i"

women sawn in halves redouble
aces becometh fives
and we're bemused by politics
magic? how fly thy lies!

Alas New York

alas new york, I knew you incognito
went to moma, ate a bad burrito
finite jest? excellent fantasy?
flashes of merriment? the lady's chamber?
make me laugh at that you camelot
the streets are full of smoke, but I cannot
un-nipped by culex tarsalis mosquito
surviving i've awarded you a veto

Nostalgia

i asked the shaman once "why was"
he swithered, then replied, "because"
he twirled his beard most mystically
then left me with the mystery
of how an ache gives rise to pain
and why the past won't come again

The Great Catharsis

(tune Betsey from Pike)

there was a car crumpled up most peacefully
under paree europe's capital city
ensanguined within it was our Princess Di
and her lover named Dodi, for them we did cry

too really
too rely
in that great calamity
Dodi and Di died

their bodies were taken to a local hospital
where they were both said to be dead on arrival
but even with certified tags on their toes
conspiracy theorists arrived in their droves

too really
too rely
but that they were dead
very few could deny

except Dodi's father who thought they had went
up in a spaceship which Elvis had sent
to live out their deaths in a bus on the moon
unless granted citizenship he surely would swoon

too really
too rely
upon that demand
many lawyers still thrive

but now there's a message from dwarf planet Xena
Tom Cruise has announced something even obscener
sages on Mars and advanced epistemology
will soon be confronted by his scientology

too really
too rely
may all such locutions
evoke a small sigh

Trend

i asked the shaman too "why bother"
he answered "seek another cover"
his message left me in a dwam
now't's climate change
which keeps me warm

How to Make Friends

if you want us to like you
stop blowing up trains
take off the disguises
we think are insane
accept that the future's
EU regulations
smile, make eye contact
in underground stations

Proposal for a Sustainable Development

every day the grass doth grow
every week a man doth mow
why not take the summer off
in the interests of sloth?

Dentistry

do you not find that
when you brush your teeth
that there's less back there
than you used to eat with
where once there were molars
behind in your jaw
it is now with incisors
that you have to chaw

To Mr Blunket's Dog

i think that i shall never see
New Labour's Home Secretary
this blessing's slightly mixed, so be
it's certain he will not see me

A Pacifist Reflects

an army not allowed to fight
seems strong, but doesn't know its might
and that means every twenty years
there must be war, or there'll be tears

not just for new fallen dead
or incompetents who led
unseasoned soldiers into war
which they had never seen before

humankind is not kept down
by law or morals, nought profound
it's saying "stop that" to your foes
and when they don't, punching their nose

however much one may want peace
life's short, and it's beyond our reach

Misanthropy

why do i not like other people
well, you too may have explored your steeple
up there with the rats
and the crap and the bats
it's not where you'd look for an equal

Age of Criminal Responsibility

she had reached the end of betweens
the elevens and twelves and thirteens
but now that a prison
is within her vision
there's a goal! and an aim!
it's sixteen

Sweet Dreams in the Rain

the ghost soldiers march 'cross the meadow
while i rest my head on my pillow
the vision's bucolic
although alcoholic
i must say that it's nice feeling mellow

Exile

on roads which lead to and from Rome
one direction is never well known
for few will require
or elsewise conspire
to find you one which will lead home

Multiculturalism

if you think that god is named allah
there's yaweh and also ishvara
izangi from the east
tian gong for chinese
too many for scotsmen to swalla

A Sundae Dressing

best recent cartoon that i've seen
is muhamet dressed up like a djinn
the cartoon may be danish
and very inflamish
but the dollop on top's like whipped cream

An Islamic Prayer

head down on the ground facing mecca
bum up like a cesspool inspector
so that when you break wind
and confess you have sinned
you'll look slightly less like a world wrecker

The Path Less Travelled by

a brimstone on the road to hell
reads pithy, states it's message well
it says go slightly back
skipping both line and crack
take advice?
no, just ignore the smell

Climate Change

a pregnant young lass from Khartoum
wore a burka designed to go boom
for with christ she had flirted
misbehaved, then converted
and we all know mood backwards
spells doom

Sustainable Consumption

a brontosaur munching on trees
thought gee whiz i must be the bee's knees
for the carbon i eat
and then later excrete
must be equal
so that's the greens pleased

Forever Wexford

writing limericks is a disease
succumb young—
there is no reprise
keep on with this shite
for the rest of your life
'cause it's nice to die shooting debris

The Theory of Religion

mankind's never followed a prophet
unless they've a line on his docket
and his bill of lading
has others persuading
that landing him
will fill their pocket

On the Virtues of an Italian Victory at the World Cup, 2006

somebody seems to have sinned
so four football clubs have been binned
to the second division
which isn't oblivion
though it might have been
had they not won

The End of Everything

Fukuyama's put mankind to bed
half past yesterday
its essence fled
the strife 'twixt the sex
death and ego complex
war and politics
all's been gainsaid

Wisdom

the fate which befalls the well read
is to find that most things have been said
so if you're up all night
scribbling great thoughts and shite
just be glad when you wake you're not dead

Eternal Verities

there's nothing which makes too much sense
unless you accept the pretence
that there is meaning
in family and breeding
then pounds count, not shillings and pence

Mindlessness

nobody's wanting to think
which is why us wise men turn to drink
it has not yet been banned
(legislation's in hand)
for the blind a nod's good as a wink

On the Death of a Maiden Aunt

the sad thing about Auntie Annie
is that she never ever got any
there was some gossip
specula philosophic
but the truth is she just wasn't randy

News Sans Publicités

sound-bytes are quite short and concise
and all of them say something nice
so that you and me
and the BBC
can have them without paying twice

Democracy

there's isms, religions and doubt
a twisting our minds all about
whatever the fetter
democracy's better
for the mob has least nous but most clout

Environmental Misanthropy

Everything's natural 'cept man.
Elephants, paramecia, ptarmigan.
A shrew lets a fart
greenhouse gasses get out—
since it t'wernt us, no one gives a damn.

Hedges

if you must have a President Bush
then it's good to have one giant tush
so there's somewhere to shove him
although you must love him
once in you can give the big push

This Amazing Body

there is a small hair on my nose
though i twiddle at
it never goes
when i wake up at night
and switch on the light
it's still there, though i can't feel my toes

The Whiff of Escape

the world is not going to hell
it is already there, hence the smell
aroma self righteous
foetid inside us
scintilla of 5 from Chanel

www.ingramcontent.com/pod-product-compliance
Ingram Content Group UK Ltd.
Pitfield, Milton Keynes, MK11 3LW, UK
UKHW021004200726
13857UKWH00004B/1266